Kid's Box

Pupil's Book 2

Caroline Nixon & Michael Tomlinson

CAMBRIDGE
UNIVERSITY PRESS

1 Hello again!

1 Listen and point.
CD1

What's your name?
How old are you?

Grandma Star

Stella

Simon

Grandpa Star

Mr Star

Mrs Star

Suzy

2 Listen, point and repeat.
CD1

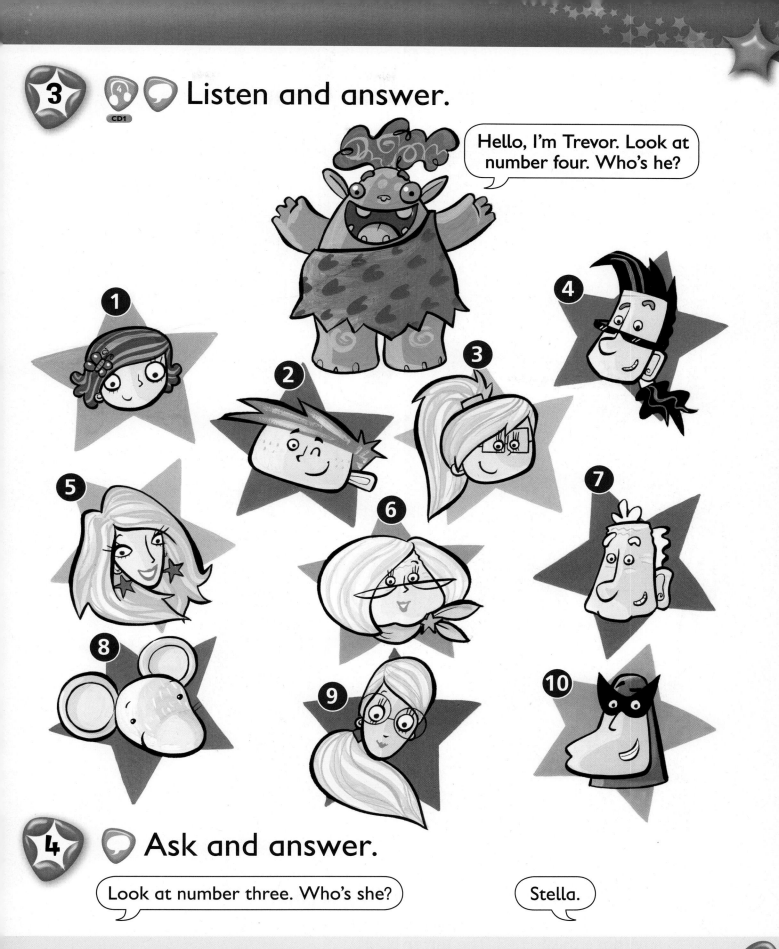

Hello, I'm Trevor. Look at number four. Who's he?

4 💬 Ask and answer.

Look at number three. Who's she?

Stella.

Suzy   Simon   Stella   Mr Star   Mrs Star   Grandpa Star   Grandma Star
What's your name?   How old are you?   Who's he / she?

5 Listen and point. Chant.

a b c d
e f g
h i j k
l m n o p
q r s
t u v
w x y z

6 Point, ask and answer.

What's this? | The letter b.

pink

grey green

orange red brown

white blue

yellow black

purple

Can you spell 'purple'?

P-u-r-p-l-e.

A

Adam ant

A sad cat in a black bag.

10 **Say and answer.**

The pencil is under the chair.

a

h

j

k

2 Back to school

1 CD1 13 Listen and point.

board

cupboard

teacher

bookcase

ruler

desk

2 CD1 14 Listen, point and repeat.

Listen and point. Chant.

School, school. This is the Numbers School.

11   Eleven desks,
12   Twelve erasers,
13   Thirteen rulers,
14   Fourteen cupboards,
15   Fifteen classrooms,
16   Sixteen teachers,
17   Seventeen pens,
18   Eighteen boards,
19   Nineteen pencils,
20   Twenty tables.

School, school. This is the Numbers School.

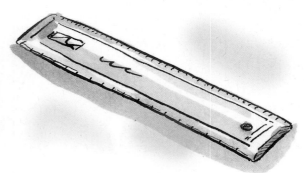

4 Ask and answer.

How many desks are there?   11

board   bookcase   cupboard   desk   ruler   teacher

This is my classroom. How many desks are there? There are a lot of desks. That's my desk next to the bookcase. There's a long pink ruler on it. There are a lot of books in the bookcase. There's a big whiteboard on the wall. There's a computer, but there isn't a television.

6 **Listen, point and repeat.**

How many … are there?   There is …   There are …

There are pencils in the classroom, yes there are.
There's a cupboard on the pencils, yes there is.
There's a ruler on the cupboard,
There's a bookcase on the ruler,
There's a teacher on the bookcase, yes there is ...

8 Ask and answer.

Where's the cupboard?   On the pencils.

I

Ingrid insect

Six big pink fish sitting in the kitchen.

10 **Say and correct.**

There are 15 pencils in the classroom.

No, there aren't. There are 16 pencils.

11 **(25)** **Listen to the story.**

1. OK, everybody. This bag is for school. Let's look.

OK, Marie!

2. Hmm. Is there a ruler?

Yes, there is. It's a 'Maskman' ruler.

3. Look, Marie. Here's an eraser.

Good! Can you put it in the bag, please, Monty?

4. Now there's an eraser in the bag, Marie.

Good! Thank you, Monty.

5. Now, how many pencils are there?

There are 9, 10, 11 pencils.

6. 11 pencils! Where's the pencil? Trevor!

Sorry. Here you are. Pencils are my favourite food.

12 **(26)** **Listen and say 'yes' or 'no'.**

3 Play time!

1  Listen and point.

Toys 4 U

kite

watch

camera

lorry

robot

computer game

2 Listen, point and repeat.

14

3 Listen, point and say the number.

These are dolls. | 19   This is a robot. | 17

4 Listen and say 'yes' or 'no'.

camera   computer game   kite   lorry   robot   watch

Whose is this jacket? …
What? That black jacket?
Yes, this black jacket.
Whose is this jacket?
It's John's.
Oh!

Whose are these shoes? …
What? Those blue shoes?
Yes, these blue shoes.
Whose are these shoes?
They're Sheila's.
Oh!

Whose is this skirt? …
What? That purple skirt?
Yes, this purple skirt.
Whose is this skirt?
It's Sue's.
Oh!

Whose are these trousers? …
What? Those brown trousers?
Yes, these brown trousers.
Whose are these trousers?
They're Tom's.
Oh!

8 **Ask and answer.**

Whose is this jacket?   It's John's.

W

Wendy whale

Where's the woman with the white watch?

10 Ask and answer.

11. Whose is this nose?

It's Simon's.

12. Whose are these eyes?

They're Stella's.

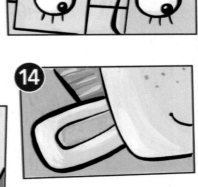

1

Whose is this robot?

It's Simon's.

2

Hello. What's your name?

My name is Metal mouth.

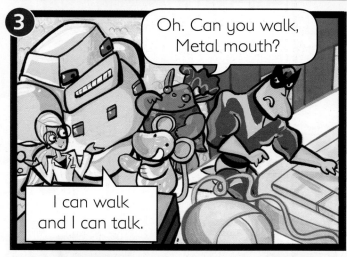

3

Oh. Can you walk, Metal mouth?

I can walk and I can talk.

4

Well, I can walk. I can talk, and I can spell. U-g-l-y.

5

I know! I know! It's ugly!

Yes, it is ... and it can't fly.

6

Maskman! Say 'sorry' please.

Sorry.

It's OK, Maskman. You're a superhero and you're Simon's favourite toy.

  Act out the story.

4 At home

mirror

mat

clock

sofa

phone

lamp

2 **Listen, point and repeat.**

20

There's a mirror in the bathroom,
And a phone in the hall.
A sofa in the living room,
A clock on the wall.
There's a lamp on the table,
And a mat next to the bed.
There's a boat in the bath,
And the boat is red.

4 Listen and correct.

clock   lamp   mat   mirror   phone   sofa

It's mine / yours.

Look at this!
Look at this!

Whose are these shoes? …
Stella! Are they yours? …
No, they aren't mine! …

Hmm. Which shoes are Simon's? …
Which, which, which, which?
Which shoes are Simon's?
The grey ones are his …

Hmm. Which shoes are Suzy's? …
Which, which, which, which?
Which shoes are Suzy's?
The red ones are hers …

SO! Whose shoes are those? …
Whose, whose, whose, whose?
Whose shoes are those?
Those are Grandpa's …
Grandpa's?

GRANDPA!

8 Ask and answer.

Which bag is yours?   The red one is mine.

E

Ellie elephant

Seven pets in seven beds.
Ten elephants with big heads.

10 Find your partner.

Are these trousers yours or mine?

They're mine.

11  Listen to the story.

1 Let's play hide and seek.

Trevor, close your eyes and count to 20.

2 … 17, 18, 19, 20. I'm coming.

3 Where are they? Whose is that tail? Ha ha! I can see you, Monty. You're under the armchair.

OK. Well done, Trevor.

4 Look. Whose feet are those? Come out, Maskman. We can see you next to the bookcase.

5 Now, where's Marie?

Marie's in the cupboard. Look! That's her hair.

6 Eeeek! What's that?

It's a toy horse.

I win!

12 Answer the questions.

Our world

1 🎧 👂 **Listen and point.**

①
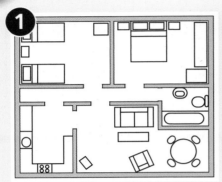

②

③

④

snow

⑤

CANADA

U.S.A.

2 🔍 **Match the text.**

a Hello. My name's Shari. I'm nine. I'm from Canada. I'm a Canadian Inuit. Here's a photo of me.

b Our house is small. It's got a hall, two bedrooms and a bathroom. There's a kitchen and a living room.

c This is a photo of the living room. There's a sofa and a table. We can watch TV here.

d This is my bedroom. There are two beds and a small chair. I've got a cupboard in my bedroom.

e My grandfather can make a house with snow. 'House' in our language is 'igloo'. This is a photo of my grandfather making an igloo.

3 ✂ Make a book.

1

Think of a house.

2

Draw pictures.

3

Write about your house.

4

Cut out photographs.

5

Make and read your book.

1 🎧55 CD1 👂 Listen and point.

Park

mummy

daddy

grandpa

grandma

baby

cousin

2 🎧56 CD1 💬 Listen, point and repeat.

3 🎧 (57) CD1 💬 Listen and answer.

4 💬 Say and answer.

He's Lenny's father.

She's Ben's mother.

Nick.

Anna.

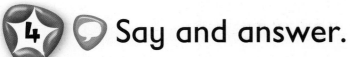

baby   cousin   mummy   daddy   grandma   grandpa

5 🎧 **58** 💬 Listen and say the number.

6 💬 Make sentences. Use the words in the box.

The dog's getting the ball.

| getting | throwing | catching | flying | talking | jumping |
| sitting | hitting | cleaning | running | kicking | sleeping |

catch   clean   fly   get   hit   jump   run   sleep   throw

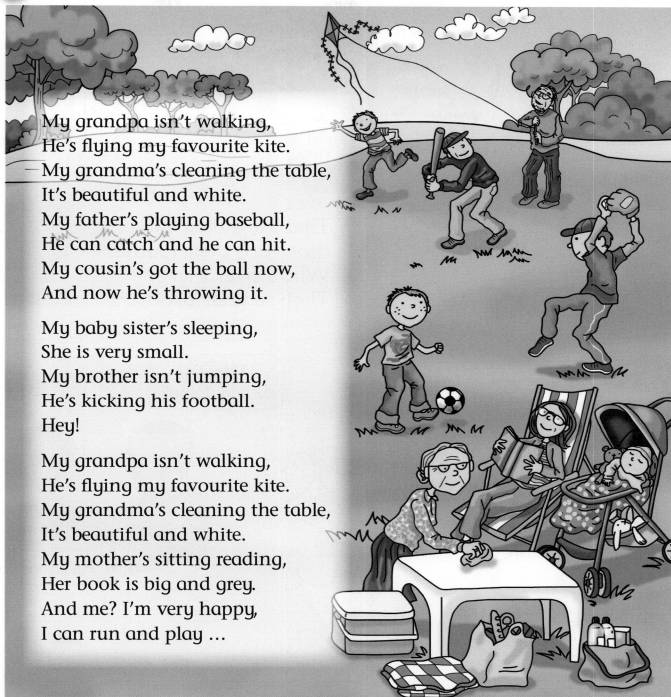

My grandpa isn't walking,
He's flying my favourite kite.
My grandma's cleaning the table,
It's beautiful and white.
My father's playing baseball,
He can catch and he can hit.
My cousin's got the ball now,
And now he's throwing it.

My baby sister's sleeping,
She is very small.
My brother isn't jumping,
He's kicking his football.
Hey!

My grandpa isn't walking,
He's flying my favourite kite.
My grandma's cleaning the table,
It's beautiful and white.
My mother's sitting reading,
Her book is big and grey.
And me? I'm very happy,
I can run and play …

8 💬 Ask and answer.

What's grandpa doing?   He's flying a kite.

'Th'

Heather the feathered friend

These are their fathers, those are their mothers. Who's over there? They're their brothers.

10 Ask and answer.

What's Simon doing?

He's sleeping.

1

Ooh! What's he doing to those shoes, Marie?

He's cleaning them, Trevor.

2

Hello, Trevor! Look at me! I'm driving Suzy's yellow lorry.

3

Hello, Maskman. What are you doing?

I'm flying my helicopter. I'm a superhero.

4

Hello, Marie. What are you doing?

I'm cleaning my shoes.

5

What are you doing, Trevor?

I'm cleaning the doll's house.

6

Oh no!

 12 Listen and say the number.

6 Dinner time

1 Listen and point.

bread
rice
juice
water
eggs
milk
chips
chicken

2 Listen, point and repeat.

3  **Listen and point. Sing.**

It's morning, it's morning.
We're having breakfast with our mum.
Bread and milk, bread and milk.
It's morning, it's morning.

It's lunchtime, it's lunchtime.
We're having lunch with our friends.
Egg and chips, egg and chips.
It's lunchtime, it's lunchtime.

It's afternoon, it's afternoon.
We're having tea in the garden.
Chocolate cake, chocolate cake.
We're having tea in the afternoon.

It's evening, it's evening.
We're having dinner with mum and dad.
Chicken and rice, chicken and rice.
It's evening, it's evening …

 4 **Point, ask and answer.**

(What's this?) (It's chocolate cake.) (What are these?) (They're chips.)

bread   chicken   chips   eggs   juice   milk   rice   water

Can I have some brown bread, please?

Here you are.

6 Listen, point and repeat.

Can I have some … ? Here you are.

7 Play bingo.

 8 Read and answer.

Hello. My name's Alex. I'm Simon's friend. It's

lunchtime and I'm having and ⊿ for lunch.

🐟 isn't my favourite lunch. My favourite is 🍗.

In the morning my favourite breakfast is 🍅 and

🥛 , and my favourite dinner is 🥩 and 🍚 .

1 What's his favourite breakfast?
2 What's his favourite lunch?
3 What's his favourite dinner?

9 · Say it with Monty

'Ch'
Charlie chicken

Chad's in the kitchen.
He's eating chicken and chips.

10 · Ask and answer.

Can I have some bread, please?

Here you are.

1

I'm having tomatoes and carrots.

2

Can I have some apple juice, please?

3

Here you are.

Is there any chocolate cake?

4

No, there isn't, but there's some chocolate ice cream.

5

Is this orange juice yours, Monty?

No, it isn't mine. It's Marie's.

6

What are you eating, Trevor? Is it chicken?

Er, no. It isn't chicken. It's a long brown pencil.

Oh, Trevor!

12 CD2 Listen and say 'yes' or 'no'.

7 At the farm

1 🎧 CD2 11 👆 Listen and point.

sheep

cow

spider

goat

duck

lizard

frog

Entry

2 🎧 CD2 12 💬 Listen, point and repeat.

40

3   Listen and point. Sing.

Cows in the kitchen, moo moo moo
Cows in the kitchen.
There are cows in the kitchen, moo moo moo
What can we do John Farmer?

Sheep in the bedroom, baa baa baa …

Ducks on the armchair, quack quack quack …

Frogs in the bathroom, croak croak croak …

Chickens in the cupboard, cluck cluck cluck …

 4 Ask and answer.

Where are the cows?   In the kitchen.

cow   duck   frog   goat   lizard   sheep   spider

6 Listen, point and repeat.

I love dogs.   So do I.   I don't.

Listen and point. Chant.

I love watermelon.	So do I.
I love pineapple.	So do I.
I love bananas.	So do I.
I love oranges.	So do I.
I love coconuts.	So do I.
I love lemon and lime.	Hmm. So do I.
I love onions.	I don't. Goodbye.

8 Say and answer.

I love cats. So do I. I love mice. I don't.

'Sh'

Shirley sheep

She shows shoes
in the shoe shop.

10 Say and answer.

They're small and green.
They've got short legs and a long tail.

Lizards.

11 Listen to the story.

1

Trevor! Pssst! Are you sleeping?

Yes, I am.

2

Trevor! Maskman! Can you be quiet, please? I'm trying to sleep!

3

I can't sleep.

Well, count sheep, Maskman.

4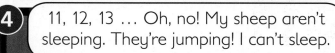

11, 12, 13 … Oh, no! My sheep aren't sleeping. They're jumping! I can't sleep.

We can't sleep now!

5

OK, let's talk about farms. Farm dogs can get sheep. Farm cats can catch mice. And we get milk from cows.

Yes … yes, I know. Maskman!

6

What are you doing, Maskman?

I'm sleeping, Marie. Goodnight.

12 Act out the story.

8 My town

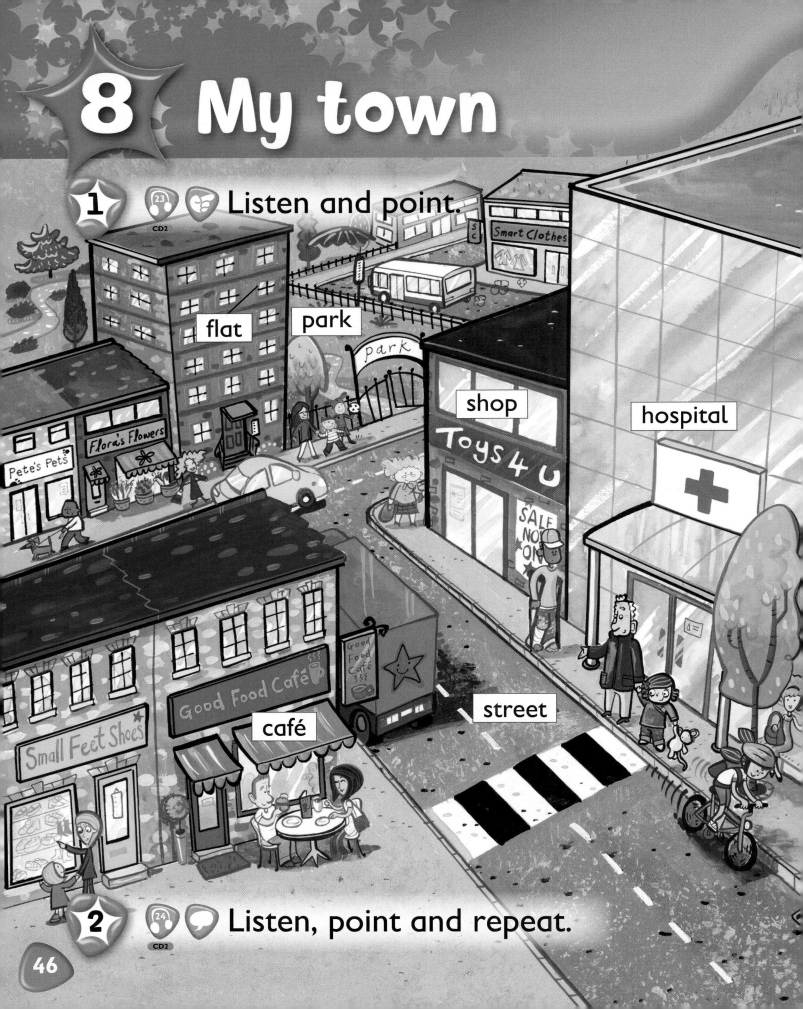

1 Listen and point.

flat

park

shop

hospital

café

street

2 Listen, point and repeat.

3 Read and answer.

1. Where's the woman with the baby?
2. How many pineapples are there?
3. How many cats are there?
4. Where's the boy with the kite?
5. What colour are the shoes in the shoe shop?
6. Where are the lemons?
7. What colour's the bus?

4 Ask and answer. Use the words in the box.

| cars men women children bikes dogs |
| babies pineapples coconuts lemons cats |

How many cars are there?   There are three cars.

café   flat   hospital   park   shop   street

5   # Listen and point.

Lenny's mum's in front of me.

 6 # Ask and answer.

Who's next to Grandma?   Grandpa.

behind   between   in front of   next to

7   **Listen and point. Sing.**

Put two books on the table …
Put a pencil between the books …
Put a pencil behind your head …
Put a book in front of your nose …
Put a book under your chair …
Put a pencil behind your ear …
Put two books on your head …
Put them all back on the table,
And now, now, sit down.

8 **Ask and answer.**

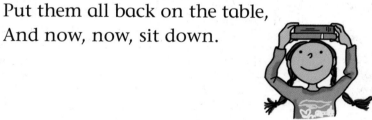

Where's the blue book?   On the sofa.

49

O

Ollie octopus

The clock's on an orange box in Tom's shop.

10 Ask and answer.

Where's the car?

It's in front of the toy shop.

1

Aaagh! Look behind you. It's behind you!

Ooooh! I can't look!

2

Oh, no. It's 'Dogzilla', the monster dog.

3

I'm coming, children.

Maskman's our superhero.

4

Aaagh! Monty! Look behind you. There's a cat. It's 'Catzilla'!

Eeeek! Help! A cat!

5

Ha ha ha.

It isn't funny!

6

Look! There's a dog. It's behind you.

Eeeek! Help! There's a dog. It's 'Dogzilla'! Help!

12 Answer the questions.

1 🎧 31 CD2 👆 **Listen and point.**

1

2

3

4

5

2 🔍 **Match the text.**

a Todd is ten. He's from Australia. This is his house. Todd's house isn't in a city. There aren't any streets or shops.

b Todd's mother and father have got a big sheep farm. They've got a lot of sheep.

c Todd's family has got two dogs. Their dogs aren't pets. They can't eat or sleep in the house or play with the children. Their dogs are farm animals. Now they're running and helping to get the sheep.

d Here's a photo of Todd. There isn't a school near Todd's house. He's having a lesson on the computer! He's talking to his teacher by internet. She's correcting his exercises.

e There isn't a hospital near Todd's house so he can't see a doctor. He can talk to a doctor on the phone or the doctor can fly to Todd's house in a small plane. The doctor's plane is like a small hospital.

3 Make a city.

1

Colour the picture.

2

Cut out the pictures.

3

Write about your city.

4

Make a poster.

9 Our clothes

1 🎧35 CD2 💬 Listen and answer.

glasses

shirt

jeans

hat

handbag

dress

2 🎧36 CD2 💬 Listen, point and repeat.

54

3 Listen and point. Chant.

Handbags, glasses,
Jackets and shirts.
T-shirts, trousers,
Dresses and skirts.
Hats, jeans,
Shoes and socks.
Put them on,
They're in the box.

 4 Listen and correct.

> There's a big box with toys.

> No, there's a big box with clothes.

dress   glasses   handbag   hat   jeans   shirt

6 Listen, point and repeat.

Have you got …?   Yes, I have.   No, I haven't.
Has he/she got …?   Yes, he/she has.   No, he/she hasn't.

Listen and point. Sing.

I've got a big garden,
I've got a big house.
I've got a good friend,
A small toy mouse.
I've got you, Monty.
I've got you.

Oh, Marie!

I've got a black mask,
And a big blue car.
I've got black glasses,
I'm the Maskman star,
And I've got you, Monty.
I've got you.

Oh, Maskman!

I haven't got
Superhero clothes.
I've got purple hair,
And a big green nose,
And I've got you, Monty.
I've got you.

Oh, Trevor!

I've got you, Monty.
I've got you.

 8 Ask and answer.

Have you got a garden?   Yes, I have.

9  Say it with Monty

CD2 45

J

Jackie jaguar

John's jeans are orange.
His giraffe's jacket's green.

10 💬 Say and answer.

There's a big red car.   b

11 **46** CD2 Listen to the story.

1 Monty! Are you wearing my long white jacket and my glasses?

Yes, I am. I'm Marie Mouse.

2 Trevor! What are you wearing?

I'm wearing blue trousers, a blue shirt, a blue hat and a black mask. Who am I?

3 I can swim and fly, but I can't sing or dance. I'm … Masktroll!

4 Look at Maskman!

5 Maskman! Are you eating a pencil?

Yes, I am. Who am I?

6 You're … Trollman!

That's right! I can't swim and I can't spell.

No, you can't, Trollman, but you've got a lot of friends.

12 **47** CD2 Listen and say the number.

10 Our hobbies

1 Listen and answer.

badminton

table tennis

painting

hockey

basketball

Sports

baseball

2 Listen, point and repeat.

3 🎧 51 CD2 💬 Listen and say the hobby.

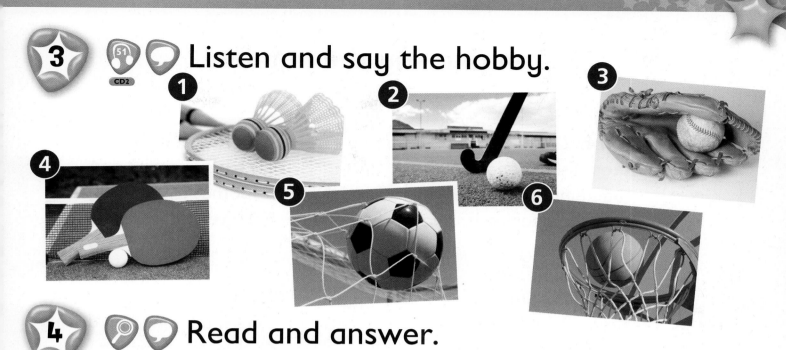

1 2 3
4 5 6

4 🔍💬 Read and answer.

These children are playing football. This sport has got two names: football and soccer. In a soccer team there are ten players who can run and kick the ball and one player who can kick and catch the ball. This player is the goalkeeper. Can you see the goalkeeper in this picture? She's wearing an orange T-shirt and black trousers.

1 We say
   a) football and badminton.
   b) football and basketball.
   c) football and soccer.

2 Eleven players can
   a) kick the ball.
   b) catch the ball.
   c) bounce the ball.

3 One player can
   a) run.
   b) bounce the ball.
   c) catch the ball.

paint   play badminton / baseball / basketball / hockey / table tennis

5   **Listen and say the number.**

1

Name: Grandpa Star
Likes: fishing and badminton
Dislikes: cleaning his shoes

2

Name: Lenny
Likes: swimming and football
Dislikes: table tennis

3

Name: Mr Star
Likes: the guitar and cooking
Dislikes: horses

4

Name: Grandma Star
Likes: painting and driving
Dislikes: gardening

5

Name: Meera
Likes: bikes and photos
Dislikes: TV

6

Name: Alex
Likes: badminton and the piano
Dislikes: baseball

7

Name: Simon
Likes: basketball and hockey
Dislikes: cleaning his room

8

Name: Mrs Star
Likes: horses and reading
Dislikes: cooking

9

Name: Suzy
Likes: singing and drawing
Dislikes: soccer

10

Name: Stella
Likes: the piano and reading
Dislikes: doing sport

I like / love …ing.   I don't like …ing.

I ❤ ❤ fishing,
I ❤ ❤ flying kites,
I ❤ taking photos,
I ❤ riding bikes.
I ❤ ❤ fishing!
Bedum ... bedoo.

I ❤ ❤ swimming,
Playing hockey too,
And I ❤ ❤ painting,
With the colour blue.
I ❤ ❤ swimming!
Bedum ... bedoo.

I ✗ driving,
Or flying in a plane,
I ✗ cleaning shoes,
I ✗ running for a train!
Bedum ... bedoo.

I ✗ cooking,
Or playing the guitar,
I ✗ badminton,
Or cleaning my dad's car.
I ✗ it!
Bedum ... bedoo.

7 **Ask and answer.**

Does Simon like painting?   Yes, he does.

R Ronny rabbit

The red robot's running with Rachel's ruler.

9 💬 Find your partner.

Do you like swimming?

Yes, I do.

Listen to the story.

Listen and say 'yes' or 'no'.

11 My birthday!

Happy Birthday Simon

cake

lemonade

sausages

watermelon

oranges

burgers

2 🎧 💬 Listen, point and repeat.
CD3

66

3 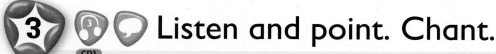 Listen and point. Chant.

Look at them
Five young men.
Look at him
He can swim.
Look at her
In her new skirt.
Look at you
And your nice clean shoe.
Look at us
On a big red bus.
Look at me
I'm under a tree.

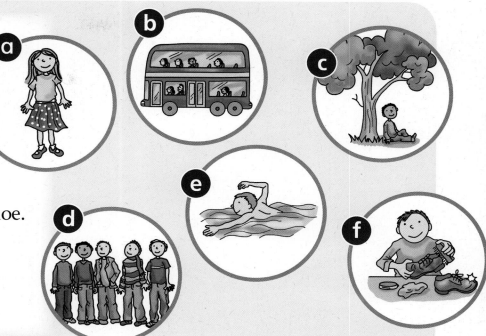

4 Read and answer.

This is 🧒's birthday party. 🧑's cooking the 🍔 and 🌭, and they're having 🥤 and 🧃 to drink. 👩's getting the fries from the 📦. 🧑🏾's taking photos. 🧒's very 😊. He's got a nice new 🚲 for his birthday. 🧒's got a big 🍀 birthday 🎂 with the number 8 on it. He's 8 today.

1. What's Mr Star cooking?
2. Who's taking photos?
3. What has Simon got?
4. What colour is his birthday cake?
5. How old is Simon?

burger cake lemonade orange sausage watermelon

5  Listen and answer.

6 Listen, point and repeat.

Would you like …?   Can I have …?   Here you are.

I'd like a great big chocolate cake,
And I'd like one for me.
I'd like a nice long sausage,
And I'd like one for me.

I'd like a burger and some fries,
And I'd like some for me.
I'd like a drink of lemonade,
And I'd like some for me.

I'd like coloured pencils, ...
I'd like a box of coloured pencils,

Don't give any to me!

8 Ask and answer.

Would you like a burger?   Yes, please.   No, thank you.

9 🔟 Say it with Monty

U

Umberto
ugly bug

The ugly duck's under the truck
and my brother's in the cupboard.

10 🔍💬 Look at the menu. Ask and answer.

What would you like to eat?

I'd like burger
and fries, please.

And what would
you like to drink?

I'd like orange
juice, please.

Menu

Food   burger
            sausages
            chicken
            fish
            fries
            tomatoes
            carrots

Drink   lemonade
            orange juice
            milk
            water

1 It's Marie's birthday today.

Let's have a party for Marie! Let's make her a pencil cake.

No, Trevor. Marie would like a lemon cake.

2 Let's have burgers and fries to eat.

No, Maskman. It isn't your birthday.

3 Now let's make the cake.

4 Ssh. Marie's coming!

Now we can't make her a cake.

5 Happy birthday, Marie!

6 Thanks, boys! Would you like to come to the café with me?

Can I have some pencil cake, please?

  12 Act out the story.

12 On holiday!

1  Listen and answer.

mountain

sun

beach

sea

shell

sand

2 Listen, point and repeat.

3 **Listen and point. Sing.**

I'm writing a new song,
I'm writing a new song.
At the beach, at the beach.

Suzy's getting lots of shells,
She's getting lots of shells.
At the beach, at the beach.

Simon's swimming in the sea,
Simon's swimming in the sea.
At the beach, at the beach.

Dad's walking on the sand,
Dad's walking on the sand.
At the beach, at the beach.

Mum's reading in the sun,
Mum's reading in the sun.
At the beach, at the beach ...

4 **Ask and answer.**

What's Stella doing?   She's writing a song.

beach   mountain   sand   sea   shell   sun

Where do you want to go on holiday?

6 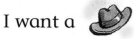 **Listen and point. Chant.**

I want a

And you want some .

She wants some

And he wants some   .

They want a

And we want a .

She wants a

And he wants a .

7 **Listen and say the letter.**

Which melon do you want? I want the big green one. m

Yolanda yak

Yes, Yolanda yak is young and yellow.

9 Ask and answer.

Do you like fishing?

No, I don't.

1 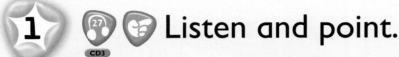 Listen and point.

1

2

3

4

2 Match the text.

a This is Jill's holiday photo. She's at the beach. The beach is black and dirty. The sea birds can't fly or swim. Jill's helping them. She wants clean beaches.

b Sue's a teacher. She's on holiday in the mountains. It's beautiful and green. She's teaching these children to speak with their hands. They are very happy!

c These children are on holiday. They're in the park. They aren't playing in the park. The park is very dirty. They're helping to clean the park.

d Julie's 19. She's on holiday here. These elephants have no family. The babies are very small. Julie's helping them. She loves animals!

3 ✂️ Make a postcard.

1

Draw a picture.

2

Write your postcard.

3

Read your postcard.

Starters practice test
Listening
Reading & writing

Part **5 questions**

 Listen and draw lines. There is one example.

31 CD3 Read the question. Listen and write a name or a number.

There are two examples.

Examples

What is the boy's name?	Tony
How old is he?	9

Questions

1 Which class is Tony in now? ....

2 What's the teacher's name? Mrs ....

3 Where does Tony live? .... Street

4 What number is the teacher's house? ....

5 How many people live in Tony's house? ....

Part ③ 5 questions

Listen and tick (✓) the box. There is one example.
What can Sam have?

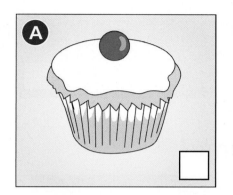

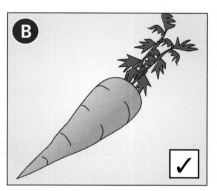

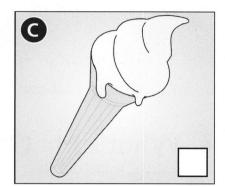

1 What does Anna want?

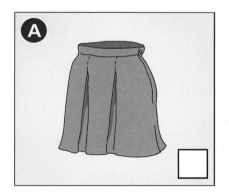

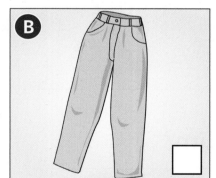

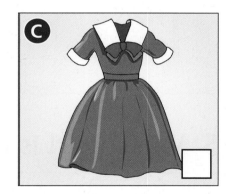

2 What's Ben drawing?

3 What's Mum doing?

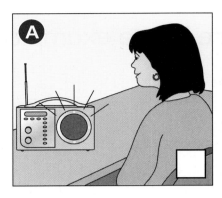

4 What's Mr Gray's favourite game?

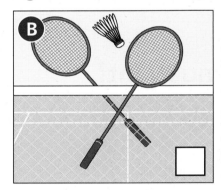

5 Which girl is Kim?

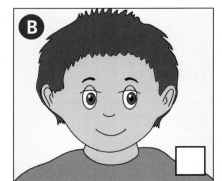

Part 4 5 questions

 Listen and colour. There is one example.

Part 5 questions

Look and read. Put a tick (✓) or a cross (✗) in the box.

There are two examples.

Examples

This is a car. ✓

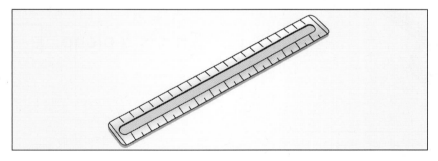

This is a pencil. ✗

Questions

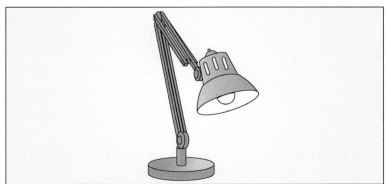

This is a lamp. ☐

2

This is a mango. ☐

3

This is a jacket. ☐

4

This is a piano. ☐

5

This is a robot. ☐

Part ⭐2 5 questions

Look and read. Write **yes** or **no**.

Examples

A girl is kicking a football. ....yes............

Two children have got kites. ....no............

Questions

1 The boys are riding bikes. ....

2 There are two ducks in the water. ....

3 The woman is painting a picture. ....

4 The baby is playing with a doll. ....

5 The man has got a black dog. ....

Part **3** 5 questions

Look at the pictures. Look at the letters.
Write the words.

Example

   <u>f</u> <u>i</u> <u>s</u> <u>h</u>

Questions

1   _ _ _ _ _

2    _ _ _ _ _

3    _ _ _ _ _ _

4    _ _ _ _ _ _

5    _ _ _ _ _ _ _

Part 4   5 questions

Read this. Choose a word from the box.
Write the correct word next to numbers 1–5.
There is one example.

A bird

I'm a small animal. I've got two

_____ legs _____ , but I haven't got

(1) _____ . I've got a

(2) _____ . I can fly and

I live in a (3) _____ in a

garden. In the morning I sing beautiful

songs. I like eating (4) _____

and small animals like spiders. I don't like

(5) _____ .

What am I? I am a bird.

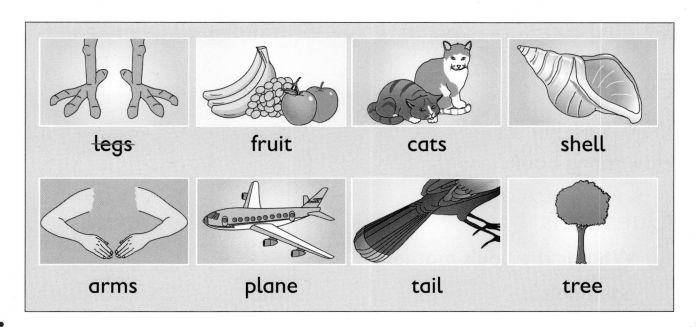

legs   fruit   cats   shell

arms   plane   tail   tree

Look at the pictures and read the questions.
Write one-word answers.

Examples

Who is having breakfast?   a .... _boy_ ....

How many books has the boy got?   .... _three_ ....

Questions

1 What is the boy's mother

pointing to?   the ....

2 What is the boy doing? --

3 Where are the girls? on the ----------------------------------

4 What is the boy doing now? --

5 Who looks angry? the ----------------------------------

Thanks and Acknowledgements

Authors' thanks

Many thanks to everyone at Cambridge University Press and in particular to:

Maria Pylas for supervising the whole project and for her unfailing good humour and support;

Susan Norris for her unflagging energy, sound editorial judgement and constant enthusiasm;

Emily Hird and Liane ('there's just one little thing ...') Grainger for all their hard work and enthusiasm;

Thanks to Mel Sharp for her wonderfully inspired and inspiring illustrations and to Melanie Williams for doing such a great job on the Teacher's Books.

And last but not least, our heartfelt thanks to Hilary Ratcliff for her sharp-eyed observations and excellent suggestions throughout the whole project and, most especially, for her skilful editing of the Teacher's Book of this cycle.

We would also like to thank all our pupils and colleagues at Star English, El Palmar, Murcia and especially Jim Kelly and Julie Woodman for their help and suggestions at various stages of the project.

Dedications

This is for my friends, Maribel Salcedo, Carmen Sánchez, Victoria Gómez and Maria Noguera, for their luminosity. – CN

To my great friends in England, who always receive us so kindly, offering their warmth and friendship: Mike and Nicola, Shaun and Lorraine and The Wheelers. – MT

The authors and publishers would like to thank the following teachers for their help in reviewing the material and for the invaluable feedback they provided:

Mira Grbic, Knjizara Cambridge Centar, Bosnia and Herzegovina; Silvia Fiorese, Cultura Inglesa, Brazil; Clara Ribeiro Haddad, Lourenço Castanho School, Brazil; Maria Teresa Sepúlveda Leiva, Universidad Santo Tomás, Chile; Milica Bilić-Štefan, Zagreb, Croatia; Nemat Matta, ELT consultant, Egypt; Catherine Johnson-Stefanidou, Johnson-Stefanidi School of Foreign Languages, Thessaloniki, Greece; Rupert Procter and Sean Fox, ABC Pathways School, Hong Kong; Sandra Fox, Gorgonzola, Italy; Hector López López, Colegio Latino Cardenas, Tabasco, Mexico; Y Paez, L Ruiz, Colegio Fernandez de Lizardi, Morelia Michoacán, Mexico; Dorota Czos, Warsaw, Poland; Katarzyna Nicholls, Teacher Trainer, Poland; Fiona Dunbar, Seville, Spain; Carmen Zahonero, Academia Aleza, Madrid Spain; Tuba Bada, Adana Gundogdu Koleji, Adana, Turkey; Celia Gaşgil, MEV Özel Izmir Ilköğretin Okulu, Izmir, Turkey.

The authors and publishers would like to thank the following consultants for their invaluable feedback:

Coralyn Bradshaw, Pippa Mayfield, Hilary Ratcliff, Melanie Williams.

We would also like to thank all the teachers who allowed us to observe their classes, and who gave up their invaluable time for interviews and focus groups.

The authors and publishers would like to thank the following for permission to reproduce photographs:

© Bryan & Cherry Alexander Photography / Alamy: p.26, © National Geographic / Getty: p. 26, © Ashley Cooper / Alamy: p.26, © Brad Simmons / Beateworks / Corbis: p.26, © George Gutenberg / Beateworks / Corbis: p.52, © Goodshoot / Corbis: p.52, © Lee Torrens / Shutterstock: p.52, © Kari Niemeläinen / Alamy: p.52, © Robert Churchill / istock: p.52, © Jean-Frédéric Ittel / Sygma / Corbis: p78, © Paul Carstairs / Alamy: p.78, © Richard T. Nowitz / Corbis: p.78, © Punchstock / Digital Vision: p.78, © Valda Tappenden / istock: p. 61, © Don Bayley / istock: p.61, © Steve Diddle / istock: p.61, © Eugenia Garcia-Valdecasas / istock: p.61, © Lewis Wright / istock: p. 61, © Oksana Struk / istock: p.61.

The authors and publishers are grateful to the following illustrators:

Melanie Sharp, c/o Sylvie Poggio; Gary Swift; Lisa Williams, c/o Sylvie Poggio; Emily Skinner, c/o Graham-Cameron Illustration; Lisa Smith, c/o Sylvie Poggio; Chris Garbutt, c/o Arena: FLP.

The authors and publishers would like to thank the children at St Matthew's Primary School, Cambridge, for participating so enthusiastically in the photograph sessions.

The publishers are grateful to the following contributors:

Gareth Boden Photography: commissioned photography
Tessa Perrett: picture research
Pentacor**big**: concept design, cover design, book design and page make-up
Melanie Sharp: cover illustration
John Green and Tim Woolf, TEFL Tapes: audio recordings
Robert Lee: song writing
Rosalie Kerr: Starters practice test